D1432040

HOW
Black
Mothers
SAY
I love you

HOW Black Mothers SAY I love you

TREY ANTHONY

Playwrights Canada Press
TORONTO

LIBRARY AND ARCHIVES CANADA CATALOGUING IN PUBLICATION
Anthony, Trey, author
        How Black mothers say I love you / Trey Anthony. -- First edition.

A play.
Issued in print and electronic formats.
ISBN 978-1-77091-802-3 (softcover).--ISBN 978-1-77091-803-0 (PDF).--
ISBN 978-1-77091-804-7 (EPUB).--ISBN 978-1-77091-805-4 (Kindle)

        I. Title.

PS8601.N73H69 2017   C812'.6   C2017-905967-X
                                             C2017-905968-8

We acknowledge the financial support of the Canada Council for the Arts, the Ontario Arts Council (OAC), the Ontario Media Development Corporation, and the Government of Canada for our publishing activities.

Canada Council   Conseil des arts
for the Arts   du Canada

ONTARIO ARTS COUNCIL
CONSEIL DES ARTS DE L'ONTARIO
an Ontario government agency
un organisme du gouvernement de l'Ontario

Ontario

Ontario Media Development
Corporation

Dedicated to my grandmothers, Daphne Dennie and Enid Maude Fraser, and my mother, Angela Senior. The fearless warriors in my life, who crossed deep and unsafe waters as acts of resistance. They showed me how to swim with my head above water. They showed me that black mothers will fearlessly perform great acts of love.

And to all the daughters who were left behind . . . we survived and we will thrive. We were and are loved.

And of course 'da beautiful girl.

I would also like to thank the Banff Playwrights Lab for giving me a safe and uninterrupted place to write. Iris Turcott, for reading draft one and two . . . I miss your brutal honesty. RIP, the coolest white chick I know. And to all the black mothers who shared their stories.

THE HISTORICAL BACKDROP OF
How Black Mothers Say I Love You

In 1955, Canada and North America introduced the West Indian Domestic Scheme. This scheme allowed eligible black women from mainly Jamaica and Barbados who were between the ages of eighteen and thirty-five, in good health, with no family ties and at least an eighth-grade education to enter Canada and parts of the US. Many women went to Canada, New York, and Miami. After one year as a domestic servant, these women were given landed-immigrant status and were able to apply for citizenship after five years. Even though the scheme originally allowed only one hundred women per year, 2,690 women had entered Canada from Jamaica and Barbados by 1965. In 1962, discriminatory language was taken out of the Canadian Immigration Act and the number of Jamaicans who came to Canada dramatically increased.

AFTER THE 1960S

Because changes in the Immigration Act allowed non-whites to enter Canada without restrictions, many Jamaicans took advantage of the opportunity and entered Canada with hopes of achieving their goals for a better life. After the purging of many racist immigration policies, a large number of Jamaicans started to enter Canada as tourists and many would later apply independently for landed-immigrant status. In the late 1960s, the Canadian government instituted the family reunification clause into its immigration policy, which made it even easier for Jamaicans and other groups to bring their loved ones to join them in Canada. Thus, during the 1970s and '80s, many Jamaicans who entered Canada were children and husbands of the Jamaican women who came to Canada between 1955 and 1965.[*]

---

[*] This article uses material from the Wikipedia article "Jamaican Canadians" (https://en.wikipedia.org/wiki/Jamaican_Canadians), which is released under the Creative Commons Attribution-Share-Alike License 3.0 (https://creativecommons.org/licenses/by-sa/3.0/).

How Black Mothers Say I Love You was first produced by Trey Anthony and Girls in Bow Ties Productions at the Factory Theatre Mainspace, Toronto, from May 5–15, 2016, with the following cast and creative team:

Daphne: Ordena Thompson
Claudette: Robinne Fanfair
Valerie: Allison Edwards-Crewe
Cloe: Jewelle Blackman

Director: Trey Anthony
Producer: Carys Lewis
Production Manager: Kimahli Powell
Stage Manager: Ashlyn Ireland
Choreographer: Irma Villafuerte
Set / Costume / Prop Design: Rachel Forbes
Set / Costume Design Assistant: Emily Butters
Lighting Designer: Steve Lucas
Composer / Sound Designer: Gavin Bradley
Outreach Coordinator: Bridget Norris-Jones
Production Assistant: Jada Crowell

The play was later remounted at Factory Theatre from February 4 through March 5, 2017, and later toured to Mississauga, Whitby, and Ottawa.

A GENERAL TIMELINE FOR THE PLAY

Daphne had Claudette in Jamaica when she was seventeen. Two years later she had Valerie.

Daphne came to the US when she was twenty-four years old, leaving behind Claudette, age seven, and Valerie, age five. After being in the US for two years she met Cloe's dad, married him and had Cloe. She was separated from her two other children for six years. By the time Valerie and Claudette came to the US, Cloe was four years old; Claudette was thirteen when she came to the US, and Valarie was eleven. Daphne was thirty years old when the girls arrived. Cloe died six years after the girls arrived at ten years old.

Claudette was nineteen years old when Cloe died and Valerie was seventeen. Daphne was thirty-six years old when Cloe died. The play begins in the present day, eighteen years after Cloe's death . . .

CHARACTERS

Daphne: Fifty-four-year-old former domestic worker from Jamaica. She has terminal cancer. She is a very religious woman. She's known for being a bit dramatic and loves to tell a good story; however, she is also a very private and proud woman.

Claudette: Thirty-seven years old, a social worker and a social activist. She is Daphne's eldest daughter. She's a pretty tomboy type who often wears a white T-shirt and a pair of jeans, occasionally she wears red lipstick.

Valerie: Thirty-five years old, married into money, but "works" at her husband's office. She is Daphne's middle daughter. She is pretty and tends to be a bit stiff and proper. She values tradition and the proper way of doing things. She tends to dress like Michelle Obama. She is the peacemaker of the family, and thus often has a nervous energy about her.

Cloe: Daphne's youngest child. She is "dead." Yet her spirit remains a constant presence in the house. Cloe is seen mainly by Daphne but felt by everyone. Cloe died when she was ten years old from sickle-cell anemia.

ACT ONE

A simple Caribbean-style kitchen in Brooklyn. In the kitchen is a table with four chairs. On the counter sits an old radio / cassette player. Soft gospel music with West Indian flavour is playing. DAPHNE, *an older West Indian black woman is in the kitchen using a mortar and pestle to pound nutmeg. She is singing along to the church hymn that is playing from the radio. She is visibly surprised when* CLAUDETTE *gingerly enters the room.* CLAUDETTE *is a black woman in her late thirties, simply dressed in blue jeans, a white T-shirt and simple black boots. She is pretty, tomboyish and wearing light lip gloss and simple earrings.* CLAUDETTE *is clutching a simple small brown suitcase.*

DAPHNE is obviously very startled.

DAPHNE
Merciful God! Claudette?

Beat.

What breeze blew you this way?

She quickly looks CLAUDETTE *up and down and wipes her hands on her apron. There is an obvious, awkward silence between them; this is not a happy family reunion.*

CLAUDETTE
Valerie called me. She told me. So I thought I should come . . .

DAPHNE shakes her head, obviously upset by this.

DAPHNE

Dat gal could never keep her mouth shut. From the time she came out of the womb she hasn't stopped talking! And I am tired of telling her whatever happens in my house, stays in MY house. See and blind, hear and deaf!

CLAUDETTE

Mom, I think someone should have told me. And if I had known I would have come sooner . . .

She looks her mother directly in the eye; DAPHNE quickly looks away. She begins pounding the nutmeg again. DAPHNE suddenly looks up and gives a quick, dismissive once-over look to CLAUDETTE.

DAPHNE

So you cut off your hair?

CLAUDETTE runs a self -conscious hand over her shortly cropped hair.

CLAUDETTE

Yep, it's been easier to manage this way.

DAPHNE shakes her head and gives CLAUDETTE a quick disappointed look and then sighs softly to herself.

DAPHNE

You use to have beautiful long hair. I don't know why you need to do all of that.

She begins pounding the nutmeg again and stops abruptly and looks up at CLAUDETTE with a disapproving look.

Everyone knows a woman's hair is her beauty.

She begins pounding the nutmeg again. CLAUDETTE *bites her lip and sighs.* DAPHNE *takes a break from the pounding and seems slightly winded.*

CLAUDETTE
Here, let me help you with that.

CLAUDETTE reaches for the mortar and pestle but stops before her hands touch her mother.

DAPHNE
I'm not dead yet. I can manage, thanks. I don't need you and Valerie running around this house acting as if I'm already dead. I may feel dead but I'm here. Surviving.

Two beats.

Not dead. Now you know who's dead? Esmee!

She hits the table for a dramatic reaction.

D-E-A-D! Dead! Poor Esmee died last month. Remember she was your Sunday-school teacher?

CLAUDETTE nods.

Well, Charlene came to pick her up for church. Remember Charlene?

CLAUDETTE looks like she's not quite sure.

You girls went to Sunday school with her? Charlene, Esmee's daughter?

CLAUDETTE
Yeah I remember her.

DAPHNE

Well, Charlene came to pick her up for Sunday service. And she wasn't waiting on the porch like she usually does. And Charlene went in and found her, in her Sunday clothes with her hat on and everything. Dead! D-E-A-D! Just like that in the kitchen. They buried poor Esmee with her hat on. A beautiful hat with a hell of a big bow! I thought that was very nice. Esmee would have liked that. She had such beautiful hats. I wanted to ask Charlene if I could possibly have a few of her hats, I'm sure Esmee wouldn't mind. But I thought that might be somewhat tasteless.

CLAUDETTE

Maybe a bit.

DAPHNE

Well you can't take it with you when you go. When I go make sure everyone knows they can just take what they want! I already told Val that anyway. She knows. Esmee should have told Charlene to give away her things but I guess the poor soul didn't know that the Lord wanted her back so soon. Poor Charlene without a mother.

She sighs to herself and shakes her head sadly.

CLAUDETTE

So how is Charlene doing?

DAPHNE

Oh as fat as ever! She got so big and fat! You know she married Cleveland. Remember Cleveland? He took you to your grade twelve prom. You would have done well if you stuck with Cleveland. He has a good job working for the government. Driving the bus! The other day I got on the bus and there he was looking very sharp in his uniform. And he didn't even let me pay, waved me away and told me to sit right at the front of the bus. Right next to him! Him and Charlene bought a house and have two good-looking boys, fair skin like their father.

CLAUDETTE
Nice. Good for them.

Sighs.

So what about you? How are you doing?

DAPHNE
Fine. Just fine thanks.

Two beats.

So are you staying? Or is this a quick visit? You could never sit still. Always rushing off to do something. So what is it this time? Where do you have to go this time?

The two women's eyes briefly meet and CLAUDETTE *looks away.*

CLAUDETTE
I'm not sure. But I think I'll stay for a while—if that's okay?

DAPHNE *is somewhat surprised.*

DAPHNE
Oh. So what about your job?

CLAUDETTE
I took a leave of absence for three months . . .

There is a tense silence as both of them contemplate what this means.

DAPHNE
Oh? Well put your things upstairs. Dinner will be ready shortly.

She begins humming and stops.

Oh the Lord is so good! I haven't been too well lately. All that garbage those doctors have been putting into my body. They think they're better than God. Pills, medicine, chemo. I lost my hair, every drop! I have less hair than you! But Val went out and got me two nice wigs. And I haven't been up to making Sunday dinner. And Valerie, bless her soul, she's been bringing over dinner, but she never puts enough coconut cream in the rice. The rice could nearly scratch your throat.

She makes a dramatic clucking sound with her throat.

But I don't want to hurt her feelings so I eat it anyways. And this morning, the Lord whispered to me today that you were coming! And one mind just said, Daphne get up and cook some dinner and make some carrot juice! Remember how much you loved my carrot juice? It was your favourite!

She beams at CLAUDETTE.

CLAUDETTE
No, that was Cloe. Not me. I hate carrot juice.

A pained look passes between them. DAPHNE looks down obviously embarrassed.

DAPHNE
Well, put your things upstairs. I'll call Val and let her know that you're here.

Lights dim. As they fade, the chorus / CLOE enters, singing a soft lullaby. DAPHNE discreetly follows CLOE with her eyes, but CLAUDETTE does not see her.

Lights up on VALERIE *and* CLAUDETTE. *The two sisters are sitting closely on a couch laughing. There is closeness and familiarity that is obvious between them, yet* VALERIE *presents a stark contrast to* CLAUDETTE. *VALERIE is a formally dressed, well put together black woman, with a long flowing weave and makeup. She smells like money; her expensive high heels and Chanel bag are casually sprawled on the ground.*

VALERIE
So I said, Mrs. Dunberry, of course you can speak to my boss. But I must let you know, he's not only my boss, he's also my husband. So, unless we're getting a divorce I don't think he's firing me! You should have seen her face! Oh yeah, this little black girl is married to the big white boss!

CLAUDETTE laughs.

CLAUDETTE
You're a trip! You kill me!

CLAUDETTE giggles some more to herself.

So how's David?

VALERIE
Good. Still a workaholic. He just bought another old building down in Harlem. He's going to tear it down and then build some lofts. It's amazing what they do to those junky old buildings.

CLAUDETTE

Junky old buildings that are people's homes.

VALERIE rolls her eyes; she obviously doesn't see it this way.

VALERIE

Come on, Claude, who wants to live like that? And David said they're sitting on prime real estate; everybody wins once a developer goes in.

CLAUDETTE

Not the poor folks. And, Val, you really believe that folks aren't upset about losing their homes?

VALERIE

Well David said—

CLAUDETTE

Oh enough about David!

Valerie

Hey, he's my husband, and I know you two don't often see eye to eye, but he's been amazing since Mom's been sick. I haven't stepped foot into the office. He understands that Mom needs me . . .

VALERIE gets a little teary. The two sisters instinctively reach for each other's hands at the same time, and VALERIE offers a grateful and weary smile.

Beat.

So glad you're back. God I missed you.

CLAUDETTE

I've missed you too.

Beat.

VALERIE
So how's your job?

CLAUDETTE
Good! Actually GREAT! I got offered a management position but I turned it down. I don't want to be in some fancy office figuring out schedules and payrolls totally removed from the kids. I got into this so I could be around those damn rude kids!

She laughs.

But I love them and I get them.

VALERIE nods her head but it is obvious that she thinks CLAUDETTE should be doing something different with her life.

You know, how would you be? Being fifteen years old and having some deadbeat mom hooked on crack, or your father beating the shit out of you, or—

CLAUDETTE sighs.

VALERIE
I don't know how you do it. Not my cup of tea. But you've always loved kids. You would have been a great mom.

CLAUDETTE
Last time I checked I still had a uterus.

VALERIE looks somewhat uncomfortable. CLAUDETTE is enjoying watching her sister squirm.

VALERIE
I'm sorry, I guess with you know—I just thought . . .

CLAUDETTE
It's cool, Val. I'm not even sure if I want kids—thought about it but we'll see.

VALERIE

Well, you're no spring chicken so you better get on it. Find you a young hot stud with some good swimmers to fertilize those old eggs! I need to be an auntie!

CLAUDETTE laughs.

CLAUDETTE

A hot young stud?

VALERIE

Well the last time I checked you still need sperm! So get on it, old girl!

CLAUDETTE

Old girl? Really! Well, you're no young hottie either! What are you and David waiting on? I'm sure Mom would be happy to have some light skin grandkids with all of that *(mimicking her mother)* "good hair" running around!

VALERIE smiles weakly.

VALERIE

Timing isn't right, I guess. And with Mom being sick it was a lot on me. But you're here now so it will make things a bit easier. Three years is too long to be away from your family.

CLAUDETTE

I know.

Beat.

You should have told me sooner. How is she really doing?

VALERIE

Not good.

She sighs.

She stopped taking the chemotherapy. It was making her really sick. She looked terrible. Throwing up. Lost her appetite. And her hair just all fell out one morning. It wasn't even gradual. It just all came out in her hand. I found her in the bathroom just sitting on the edge of the tub with her hair in her hands crying. I was so scared, Claudette. I've only seen Mom cry twice. The day Cloe died and then at Cloe's funeral.

Beat.

And I think losing her hair, that was it for Mom. She just said no more. Her body has had enough. And she said if anyone's going to save her it's God. So she has her prayer meeting nearly three times a week and the pastor and the entire church prays for her every Sunday, and also at the evening and weekly services.

CLAUDETTE
That's where she is now?

VALERIE
Yeah. But it's only a matter of time. She's dying. She knows it. But she's been great. She's handling it. She's made out her will and put me on all her bank accounts. She's got a dress and she's been trying to find a nice hat.

CLAUDETTE
Yeah I heard about the hat!

VALERIE
Miss Esmee? She told you about her hat? Of course she did! Oh it was awful, Claudette! At her funeral she had on a lime-green dress with taffeta underneath and a lilac hat with this huge bow on it. And because she was lying in the coffin, it was sort of lopsided and falling over one eye. And I had this awful urge to just sit her up for a minute so I could put her hat on straight. And now Mom has requested that she wants a lilac hat just like Esmee. And how wonderful Esmee looked in her coffin. It was the talk of the church, what a beautiful hat Esmee had! So you know Mom, she doesn't want to be outdone by Miss Esmee, not even in death! So we have been

in every hat shop in New York looking for a hat. And Mom keeps saying, *(mimicking her mother)* "No, Valerie, that's not the hat. Esmee's bow was much bigger! We have to keep looking!"

They both burst out laughing. They sit in silence side by side for a while holding hands.

Two beats.

She went last week to look at the plot of land beside Cloe. When Cloe died she bought the plot right beside her. She wants to be buried there.

CLAUDETTE
Figures. Together even in death.

VALERIE
Claudette, come on . . .

CLAUDETTE abruptly gets up from the couch and starts pacing the room.

CLAUDETTE
No, you were in this house too, okay! *(mimicking her mother)* "Girls, don't play too loudly, you know your sister is sick and the noise disturbs her. No, Mom can't come to your school play because Cloe is in the hospital. No, you can't get that new bike because Mom has just spent the money to buy a ventilator for Cloe's room. So you and Val share a room because your sister doesn't need your germs around her. Dear God, why are you children so selfish? Can't you girls think about your poor sister for once!"

VALERIE gets up to try and calm CLAUDETTE down. She reaches out to gently touch her.

VALERIE
Claude, you just got here, don't do this—

CLAUDETTE
No.

She shrugs off VALERIE's hand.

The only thing she ever cared about was Cloe! Cloe, Cloe, Cloe! And I thought that once she was dead we could finally have a mom! A real mom. And even now that she's dead, she still wants her! Take her, Cloe; you can have her! She's all yours again!

Two beats. CLOE enters the room slowly. The girls sense her but do not see her.

She stopped taking the fucking treatment because she'd rather be with Cloe than stay here and fight and be with us!

VALERIE
Claudette, that's not true! She tried! The treatment was making her sick, that's why she stopped. She wants to live! She wants to be here! So that's not true!

CLAUDETTE
Really? Not true, Val? Or you don't want it to be true?

The room is filled with tension as VALERIE ponders this. Suddenly DAPH-NE's voice is heard off stage but we do not see her.

DAPHNE
(off stage) Girls?

CLOE makes a gentle humming sound. VALERIE and CLAUDETTE barely acknowledge her. They still don't see or hear CLOE but they sense something. Suddenly DAPHNE enters the room. She is back from church, Bible in hand. She spots the girls but primarily addresses CLOE.

Oh you're here!

DAPHNE looks at all her children, yet she beams brightly at CLOE. They both lock eyes, apparently oblivious to CLAUDETTE and VALERIE being in the room.

Lights abruptly drop to black.

Lights up. It's nighttime. VALERIE *has on her coat ready to leave.* DAPHNE *is ready for bed.* DAPHNE *walks* VALERIE *to the door.*

DAPHNE
See you tomorrow, Valley.

VALERIE
If you want me to stay over I can.

DAPHNE
Not necessary. Claudette is here, I'll be fine. And David must need you to come home sometimes.

VALERIE smiles weakly.

VALERIE
I'll bring you over some dinner tomorrow. Rice and peas and—

DAPHNE
(quickly) Val, I'm fine. Really, I'm fine!

VALERIE
Mom, I don't mind cooking and tomorrow I can make—

DAPHNE
Believe me, Val; you have done more than enough in the kitchen!

VALERIE

(a bit puzzled) Okay . . . Well, Claude, I'll see you tomorrow. Mom, get some sleep and remember your pills, I put them on the nightstand. Take them! And tomorrow for dinner, I'll—

DAPHNE shoves a stunned VALERIE quickly through the door and quickly closes it.

DAPHNE

Bye, Val!

Turning towards CLAUDETTE.

Whatever you do don't let her in the kitchen! If anything is going to kill me, it will be that girl's cooking!

Her and CLAUDETTE laugh.

Beat.

Val is glad you're back. I think having you around is good for her. I told Pastor Thomas that you were visiting; he said you should try and come to service next week, or you could come to prayer meeting on Tuesday night. We are having it at Sister Marie's house. Oh Sister Marie would be so happy to see you! She was like a second mother to you!

CLAUDETTE appears slightly agitated by DAPHNE's "second mother" reference.

CLAUDETTE

We'll see.

DAPHNE

Well Sunday it is then! We can all go together! Valerie can invite David. I couldn't tell you the last time I've seen him, he's so busy. But we can all go together to church, just like old times. Val, Cloe— I mean David.

CLAUDETTE

Mom, I don't want to go.

DAPHNE

It's not about if you want to go, Claudette, maybe you NEED to go.

CLAUDETTE *sighs deeply.*

Everyone needs a blessing and I think you NEED one. I can pray for you but—

CLAUDETTE

Mom.

DAPHNE

Fine. But Sister Marie would be so glad to see you. She's always asking for you. Did you get the scarf and the hat that she made for you? I sent it but I wasn't sure if it was the right address—you know you are always moving, on the move, on the move.

CLAUDETTE

Yeah I got it. I should have sent her a thank-you note.

DAPHNE

Yes you should have. Well that's settled then, you can thank her in person at church on Sunday.

CLAUDETTE

Do the people at church know?

DAPHNE *appears a bit taken aback but recovers quickly.*

DAPHNE

Of course, they have all been praying for me.

CLAUDETTE *sighs.*

CLAUDETTE
Not that, Mom. About me.

DAPHNE begins to busy herself by arranging the cushions on the couch, deliberately avoiding eye contact with CLAUDETTE. It is obvious that she is uncomfortable with the question.

DAPHNE
I see no reason to broadcast your business everywhere.

CLAUDETTE
Really?

It is obvious that DAPHNE wishes to change the subject and she begins to head towards the stairs.

DAPHNE
I need to go and take my pills. Good night. I'll see you in the morning.

She quickly brushes past CLAUDETTE, attempting to head upstairs.

CLAUDETTE
You know you can't keep pret—

DAPHNE
Claudette, I'm tired, *(firmly)* not now. I'm a sick woman and Val said for me to take my pills, so good night.

Beat.

CLAUDETTE
Mom . . . I—

DAPHNE
Good night, Claudette.

A dejected CLAUDETTE *turns away and heads towards the kitchen table, and a determined* DAPHNE *heads towards the stairs, but she hesitates, and seems to be conflicted.*

Claudette . . . um um . . . if you get cold there's a blanket in the closet in your room.

CLAUDETTE
Thanks.

DAPHNE, *slowly but still holding firm, heads up the stairs.*

Upstairs in her bedroom an emotional DAPHNE *reaches for her Bible on her nightstand, but begins to cry softly before she can even open it.* CLOE *enters the room; she looks concerned about her mother.* DAPHNE *sees her and smiles through her tears, grateful to see her.* DAPHNE *sighs deeply as* CLOE *walks towards her and kisses her forehead and tenderly wipes her tears.* CLOE *sits down beside her on the bed.* DAPHNE *rests her head in* CLOE's *lap and gently cries as* CLOE *sings a soft lullaby while stroking* DAPHNE's *hair.*

Lights down.

The next day. The scene opens with a well-dressed VALERIE coming through the door in a tight-fitting, sexy but elegant suit, with various bags filled with groceries. CLAUDETTE is sitting at the kitchen table eating breakfast wearing a fitted, tight, boyish undershirt; a do-rag and a pair of boxers. VALERIE eyes her critically.

VALERIE
No Victoria's Secret in Montreal?

CLAUDETTE
Saving it to wear on my wedding night!

VALERIE rolls her eyes.

VALERIE
You sleep okay?

CLAUDETTE
Not bad, but it's weird being in our room without you. I guess I've gotten used to having your snoring lull me to sleep!

She imitates VALERIE with loud, exaggerating snoring noises.

VALERIE
I don't snore! And if you miss me so much, I could always ask David if I could move back for a bit!

CLAUDETTE
Do you ask his permission for everything?

VALERIE
He's my husband.

CLAUDETTE
And?

VALERIE looks slightly annoyed.

VALERIE
It's not permission.

CLAUDETTE gives her a mocking look.

Listen, I'm not trying to burn my bra; I'll leave that one for you. And it's just the way we do things in our marriage. He just likes me to keep him informed about what I'm doing. No biggie. *(quickly)* He does the same. And it's been working for nearly six years so we must be doing something right.

She avoids CLAUDETTE's judging eyes as she begins to quickly unpack the groceries.

CLAUDETTE
You happy?

VALERIE
He's good to me.

CLAUDETTE
That's not what I asked.

VALERIE abruptly stops unpacking the groceries and looks directly at CLAUDETTE.

VALERIE

Come on, who's really happy? We're all just getting by. You go to work, cook dinner, pay bills, watch TV and when you're not tired you have sex once a week and, MAYBE, if you're really happy, have a date night once a month and take vacations twice a year with another "happy" couple who you can't stand but you vacation with them because the thought of TRULY being alone with your husband for seven days creeps you the hell out, because you both know you'll run out of things to say! That's just life! And yes, this is my so-called "happy life."

Two beats.

VALERIE sighs.

He's what I know . . . And I couldn't imagine my life without him. But it's lonely . . . I want a baby and David's suggestion was to get a dog.

CLAUDETTE

You're trying for a baby?

VALERIE

I came off the pill two years ago and I had one miscarriage.

CLAUDETTE

You had a miscarriage?

VALERIE

I don't want to talk about it, okay? We're seeing a fertility specialist; he thinks I'm stressed. And I guess this thing with Mom has really taken its toll on me. Where is she?

CLAUDETTE

Prayer meeting.

VALERIE

Good. Church is good for her.

CLAUDETTE

Well, she had on her finest. Her matching navy shoes to go with her matching navy dress with the yellow sunflowers. Our mother is quite a sharp dresser. All she needed was a matching floral Bible.

VALERIE

Claudette! You know if I didn't know better I would think Mom was having an affair with Pastor Thomas. She's always at the damn church.

CLAUDETTE

Now that would be something. All these years we were thinking our mother was some God-fearing Christian and she's really giving a hallelujah to Pastor Thomas!

VALERIE

And Pastor does have REALLY big feet!

CLAUDETTE

Oh gross! Did you need to go there?

VALERIE

You started it! And he does have big feet, size twelve!

She demonstrates with her hands.

Big! Really big!

CLAUDETTE

I'm going to throw up in my mouth!

They both burst out in a fit of uncontrollable giggles. After they have regained their composure, they sit in a comfortable silence.

Two beats.

VALERIE
So what about you . . . you happy?

CLAUDETTE
Was for a bit. But not anymore.

VALERIE
You still with um . . . your friend?

CLAUDETTE
Jenna's not my friend and you know that. She's my partner, or used to be . . .

VALERIE
You broke up?

CLAUDETTE
Yep! It's over.

VALERIE
Oh . . . Claude, I'm sorry. I know she meant a lot to you. And I won't even try to pretend that I get this . . . um "thing" between the two of you, and hey, it's none of my business, and as long as you're not throwing it in everybody's face and you're happy. Hey!

   Beat.

But with two women it must be so much easier; you automatically get each other. You can go places together; you can dress the same, borrow each other's clothes! It would be like hanging out with your best friend all day! If I was with a woman I would be just so happy!

   CLAUDETTE *looks at her with disbelief.*

CLAUDETTE
Wow! Val, every relationship has its ups and downs.

VALERIE nods.

VALERIE
Of course, but with women it has to be easier. Any chance of working it out?

CLAUDETTE
Nope. I tried but she doesn't want to. She's already met somebody else.

VALERIE
Oh . . . Well sometimes you just need a little space from each other and then you realize that there is something that needs saving. And you come back and try to work it out.

Beat.

David and I separated for three months.

CLAUDETTE
You and David broke up!

VALERIE
Shh! I didn't even tell Mom. Told no one, actually. He was spending so much time at the office, barely coming home, and I was so busy with Mom I was kind of glad that he was busy too. And then I just got this feeling that there was more to this . . . like there was someone else.

CLAUDETTE
You thought he was cheating?

VALERIE
Yep, and I was right. The sweet little co-op student, *(in a Valley girl voice)* "Sarah!" She was perky, happy, blond and eighteen. How do you compete with that?

CLAUDETTE reaches in to hug her.

CLAUDETTE
Val. I'm so sorry.

VALERIE
I used to think that I was past all of that race shit, you know. I used to think it didn't matter with me and David. We were in love and colour didn't matter. And yeah his parents were a bit stupid and you know I freaked out when his dad didn't come to our wedding, but even he came around.

She sighs.

But when I found out about the affair I was right back in grade six. Hating this nose, hating this skin, hating this hair. Thinking I bet all along all he wanted was a white woman and maybe I just wasn't enough?

CLAUDETTE
Val! You? You're brilliant, pretty, smart! You're amazing! You know that, right?

VALERIE doesn't look convinced.

You should have called me. I would have taken the first plane here, you know that?

VALERIE
You were busy with your own life and for once I needed to figure this out on my own. I couldn't keep running to my sister to figure out my life.

Beat.

And we're in counselling. And we're trying to work it out but it's hard. He just doesn't get it, you know. He keeps saying that colour has nothing to do with it! She could have been purple for all he cares! But it matters to me!

Beat.

It just wouldn't hurt so much if she was black. And our counsellor, clueless! Telling me we need to look at what was going on IN the marriage that let David look outside. But I just can't get past the fact that she was white.

CLAUDETTE
It will take a little time, give yourself some time.

VALERIE nods.

VALERIE
For months I couldn't even make him touch me. Even now I just close my eyes and think about the baby.

CLAUDETTE reaches in and hugs VALERIE.

CLAUDETTE
Do you think having a baby now is the answer?

VALERIE
I don't know . . . but I want something, you know, that really belongs to me . . .

Two beats.

Wow, enough about me! I totally hijacked that conversation. What about you?

CLAUDETTE
Where to begin.

VALERIE
You umm . . . love her?

CLAUDETTE
Madly.

VALERIE

So what's the problem?

CLAUDETTE

Me. She use to love me so much and it made me feel like I was drowning. Being swallowed up. It was too much. And something just felt like it was "missing." And she wanted us to buy a place together and I went along with it, looked at places, picked colour schemes, put down a down payment. And two days before we're about to close on the house I broke up with her. I couldn't do it.

VALERIE

Maybe you got cold feet. Buying a house together is a big commitment. Maybe you just need some more time.

CLAUDETTE

We've been together for nearly three years. Time? No. It's more than that. Something was just missing and I love her, really I do, but— Shit I don't know!

VALERIE

If it's meant to be it will be. Maybe she's not the right person. When you're ready there will be no doubt.

CLAUDETTE

With David you didn't have any doubts?

VALERIE

None. But in retrospect I think David just fitted the dream. I wanted someone to take care of me. I wanted the kids, the white picket fence, a dog named Spot. You know, the entire dream? And for a while that's what we had. And I buried my head in the sand for a long time, so I wouldn't have to see anything that interfered with the dream . . .

Two beats.

Maybe it's better to be a bit cynical about love . . . not believing that it's going to last or stick around.

CLAUDETTE
No. I don't want to be cynical or have this doubt all the time. I want to be certain. I don't want to spend my whole life questioning, is this it? Is this the "one"?

VALERIE
I thought David was the "one" and look at where that got me.

CLAUDETTE
Yeah but at least you were certain, you were sure about him.

VALERIE
Yeah.

She sighs.

You'll know when you know. Trust me, soon you'll be calling me whipped out of your mind because some little woman just turned you out!

VALERIE gets up and does a provocative little booty shake. CLAUDETTE is amused and shocked.

CLAUDETTE
Damn, Val! I didn't know you had it in you!

VALERIE
Learnt it in my Zumba class!

They both burst out laughing. There is a tender sister moment between them, as VALERIE rests her head on CLAUDETTE's shoulder—a comfort for both of them.

I was so mad at you for just leaving like that . . . I just don't get how you did that. You just leave your family and barely keep in touch?

CLAUDETTE
Is that why you didn't call when Mom got sick?

VALERIE
Yes. No . . . There was just a lot going on. But you're home now.

Beat.

Don't leave me like that again, okay?

CLAUDETTE
Promise.

They both touch the tip of their pinky fingers to their tongues and then touch each other's pinky fingers together.

VALERIE
You and me.

CLAUDETTE
Me and you . . . I'll take care of you.

They hold each other's eyes for a few seconds before CLAUDETTE, *nervous with the intimacy, breaks the stare.*

Mom should be home soon?

VALERIE
Yeah, I better start dinner. I was thinking rice, oxtail and coleslaw. Not too sure about the oxtail; the last time I made it, it was a bit chewy and—

CLAUDETTE
(quickly) I'll cook!

VALERIE

Don't be silly! You just got here; you don't want to be slaving in a kitchen all day. And with a little practise I'm sure the oxtail will turn out better, and maybe this time Mom will eat it all. The last time I think I gave her too much, but she did say it was like nothing she's ever tasted before!

VALERIE beams with pride.

CLAUDETTE

Well oxtail is my specialty. So you make the salad and I'll do the rest.

VALERIE

Well I could at least make the rice.

CLAUDETTE

No! I mean that's fine. I can do that!

VALERIE

Okay . . . I'll just do the salad.

VALERIE heads to the fridge and a relieved CLAUDETTE begins prepping food.

Lights down.

Lights up.

VALERIE, DAPHNE and CLAUDETTE are at the dinner table.

DAPHNE
That was delicious, Claudette. One of the best meals that I've had in months!

VALERIE gives DAPHNE a sharp look. DAPHNE catches herself and tries to retract the statement.

I mean it has been one of the few meals that I've been able to eat IN a while! I mean because of my sickness I've not had much of an appetite. And, Valerie, I know that you have tried . . . but God does not like a liar, so I have to be honest with you about this food business you—

CLAUDETTE saves the day!

CLAUDETTE
Mom, how was church?

DAPHNE
Church!

DAPHNE claps her hand together in glee.

I had a good talk with Pastor Thomas and he told me that I should recite Romans 11, verse 15 and 16 every night before I go to bed. In the morning splash a little bay rum in my bath and while in the bath read verses 18 through 25. When I get out of the bath I should have a boiled egg and a simple piece of toast with no butter. Sister Myrtle said to make sure I eat the egg with my right hand.

CLAUDETTE
Well . . . you're right-handed, right? So what other hand would you eat it with?

VALERIE tries to suppress a laugh and DAPHNE shoots her a bad look.

DAPHNE
Claudette, all the idle time that you have making fun of Sister Myrtle's good advice could be time spent reading your Bible.

DAPHNE looks pointedly at both of them.

Did you girls say your prayers last night?

CLAUDETTE
Nope, but I'm on it tonight, Mom!

VALERIE bursts out laughing. DAPHNE is far from impressed.

DAPHNE
As for you, Valerie. Sister Marie was asking for you. She said she couldn't remember the last time she's seen you in church. I was so embarrassed. Had to make up all kinds of excuses for you.

VALERIE
I've been a bit busy, Mom; you know that.

DAPHNE is not impressed.

DAPHNE
Hmm. And, Claudette, it would be nice for you to go and visit Sister Marie. I told her that you were here and she told me that Tamara told her you had

come by but she had missed you. She's so excited to know that you're here. You must go and see that poor woman.

DAPHNE shakes her head sadly.

She is having such a hard time with those children. You would think that they would be grateful that their poor mother sent for them. But not them! They are killing that poor woman! Their mother works two jobs for them and instead of helping his mother the boy has been running the streets. I heard he's—

She looks around the room and leans in.

(in a conspiratorial whisper) He's selling marijuana! Drugs! And her daughter, sixteen years old with a belly. Pregnant at sixteen! And poor Sister Marie under so much stress that she has lost so much weight! Claudette, you wouldn't even recognize her. Pure skin and bones! Those children are killing her!

VALERIE
MOM . . . you know she lost all that weight because she has diabetes and the doctor put her on a diet.

DAPHNE looks a bit sheepish and knows she has been caught in a lie.

DAPHNE
Well, I'm sure having a drug-dealing son and a sixteen-year-old daughter with a belly isn't helping her much!

CLAUDETTE
Is she keeping the baby?

DAPHNE
Well of course. What else would she do with it?

CLAUDETTE
She could have an abortion. A woman should have options and know them.

DAPHNE
Abortion! Nonsense! She's in the church!

CLAUDETTE
That didn't stop her from having sex.

DAPHNE
Claudette, that doesn't mean she has to continue sinning, and abortion is a sin.

VALERIE
Well maybe she could put it up for adoption. There's a lot of couples out there looking to adopt.

CLAUDETTE
White babies, not black ones.

VALERIE
I'm sure she could find a nice couple who—

DAPHNE
Hello! The child has a mother. She does not need to give away her child. This isn't a kitten—it's a child. A mother just doesn't give away her child.

CLAUDETTE
You did.

DAPHNE
I beg your pardon.

CLAUDETTE
You gave us away. You left us in Jamaica with Grandma for nearly six years while you were here.

DAPHNE

Claudette, I left you with Momma while I was up here trying to sort things out.

CLAUDETTE

It took you SIX years to sort things out?

> *DAPHNE appears pained and looks down at her hands. We hear the gentle humming of CLOE as she enters the room. DAPHNE looks past CLAUDETTE; the humming catches her attention and DAPHNE's eyes rest on CLOE.*

I guess you were sorting things out when you married Cloe's dad and had Cloe? And Cloe took our place and you forgot that you had two kids that you left behind.

> *VALERIE coughs nervously and gets up from the table. CLOE's humming slowly rises.*

VALERIE

I forgot that I had bought a delicious apple pie; who wants pie!

CLAUDETTE

Sit down! Why doesn't anyone ever want to talk in this family? Val, you were only five years old and she cried every night for you. And Momma would beat her for crying and she wouldn't stop crying. Sometimes I would hide Momma's belt so she couldn't beat her. You were five, just a baby, and I was just seven. Seven years old?

> *Two beats.*

A mother doesn't give away her children like they're kittens. You did.

> *The air is charged. CLOE's humming becomes louder and she positions herself in between DAPHNE and CLAUDETTE. CLAUDETTE does not see*

her but feels her. DAPHNE shifts her glance between both her daughters, not sure who to look at. She begins to busy herself clearing the table.

DAPHNE
I'm too tired to talk about this now, Claudette. I'm not feeling my best and that's water under the bridge. Val, could you clear the table, please. Good night, girls.

DAPHNE attempts to get up from the table.

CLAUDETTE
Please don't do this. Don't dismiss me. You never want to talk about this.

VALERIE
Enough, Claudette. Mom's tired.

CLAUDETTE
Fine.

(to VALERIE) But I want to know ONE thing. What made you think it was okay to leave your children and then think you could just pick up where you left off?

VALERIE
Claudette, not now.

DAPHNE
I tried my best to do what was right for you girls. *(firmly)* And that's that.

CLAUDETTE
That's that? You leave your kids behind and that's that.

Beat.

You came to Brooklyn because you were tired of being a mother to two little girls. So you just took a break. If this choice was about us, how come we were conveniently forgotten for nearly six years?

CLOE abruptly stops humming as DAPHNE pushes herself away from the table with renewed energy and anger.

DAPHNE
I worked three jobs when I got here. Three! And I made sure you girls had everything.

CLAUDETTE
Everything but a mother.

Two beats.

I got my period. And for three days I bled. Stuffing tissue in my underwear. I thought God was punishing me. I thought I was dying. No one told me what a period was. I was too scared to go to Momma. I didn't want her to beat me.

Beat.

Three days I bled by myself and all I wanted was a mother to tell me that I was okay, that this was okay.

DAPHNE looks at her and bows her head. CLOE comes to her and puts her hand on her shoulder to comfort her. DAPHNE is grateful for the comfort.

DAPHNE
Claudette, I . . .

She sighs.

DAPHNE falters slightly and looks visibly shaken but tries to remain strong. VALERIE can see that this conversation has taken a toll on her.

VALERIE

Mom, you need your rest. I'll help you up the stairs.

> *VALERIE gets up and shoots CLAUDETTE a disgusted look as she assists a weakened DAPHNE up the stairs, leaving a dejected CLAUDETTE at the table. CLAUDETTE begins to clear the table and CLOE flings a plate onto the floor. It shatters to pieces and CLAUDETTE is forced to acknowledge her presence. CLAUDETTE is scared; she knows CLOE is here. She feels her but doesn't see her.*

CLAUDETTE

I know you're here! But you better remember you're dead! I know what you want!

> *Two beats.*

It's her, isn't it? You want her, don't you! You want to take her again! Well for Christ's sake, she's my mom too! And I need her! I NEED her, Cloe! So leave us the hell alone!

> *VALERIE enters the room, looking shocked and puzzled. CLOE quickly brushes past CLAUDETTE, exits the room and heads up the stairs.*

VALERIE

Claudette, who are you yelling at?

CLAUDETTE

Cloe!

> *A concerned VALERIE gently steers CLAUDETTE to the couch.*

VALERIE

Claude, *(gently)* Cloe's dead. You know that.

CLAUDETTE

No, she's here. Right here; she's come for her! Val, you got to believe me she's here.

CLAUDETTE starts crying.

She is.

It is obvious that VALERIE is skeptical but she reaches in to comfort a crying CLAUDETTE.

You don't believe me, do you?

Lights down.

Lights up on VALERIE. *One week later.* CLAUDETTE *is on the phone as* VALERIE *enters the kitchen.*

CLAUDETTE
Yes, Dr. Harris, I will definitely ensure that she doesn't miss her next appointment. Thank you. Goodbye.

She slams down the phone.

I can't believe that woman!

VALERIE
What?

CLAUDETTE
Mom missed all of her doctor's appointments this week! She just never showed up. It's bad enough that she's not doing the chemo but for God's sakes, she has cancer not the flu! She needs to see a doctor!

VALERIE
Claude, what are they going to tell her that she doesn't already know? Yes, Miss Robinson, last week you were dying and this week you're still dying. At this point she should choose how she wants to spend her time.

CLAUDETTE
Things change. So she still needs to see her doctor. Just last week I was reading an article about a woman who was diagnosed with terminal brain

cancer and she tried this radical treatment, along with yoga, meditation and a raw food diet and now she's in remission!

VALERIE
So all she has to do is yoga and stop eating chicken-foot soup in exchange for a piece of lettuce and she'll be cured. Okay, I'll see if I can sell Mom on that one!

> DAPHNE *walks slowly into the room; she wears a simple house dress and clutches her Bible. She is a bit weaker than in the previous week but is trying to look stronger than she feels.*

DAPHNE
Sell me on what?

CLAUDETTE
Yoga.

DAPHNE
Yo-who?

CLAUDETTE
Yoga.

DAPHNE
What is dat?

CLAUDETTE
It's a form of exercise that increases your flexibility, helps you reduce stress and is good for you! So me and Val thought you should try it!

DAPHNE
Oh, at my age, I don't have no time for any yougoo rubbish!

VALERIE
And you obviously don't have time to go and see Dr. Harris anymore. You told us you saw her this week and everything was fine.

DAPHNE looks annoyed yet guilty.

DAPHNE
I don't need no fancy doctor to tell me anything that the Lord won't. I put my faith in God and not in man.

CLAUDETTE
You are sick and you need to see a doctor. Regularly.

DAPHNE
If and when the Lord wants to take me home there is nothing medicine, doctor or anyone can do. And I am ready! Dear Lord take me when you want!

DAPHNE stretches her arms out wide, one hand still gripping her Bible; she looks up at the ceiling and throws her head back. Then she suddenly looks accusingly at VALERIE.

The only thing holding me back is that YOU won't help me find a good hat to greet my maker at heaven's door!

CLAUDETTE
I'll help you find a hat. "THE" hat if you go and see Dr. Harris.

DAPHNE is clearly amused by CLAUDETTE's offer and chuckles to herself as she gives CLAUDETTE a quick once-over.

DAPHNE
You? Claudette, I am looking for a HAT, not a baseball cap! And I know you hate shopping, and I don't think you and I have the same . . . um . . . um . . . fashion sense.

CLAUDETTE is also slightly amused and gently teases.

CLAUDETTE
Okay, well maybe I'll leave the hat shopping to the experts, but I'll go to church on Sunday if you go and see Dr. Harris.

DAPHNE
Church! Will you wear a dress?

CLAUDETTE is taken back by this, but VALERIE shoots her a quick look.

CLAUDETTE
I'll wear a . . . dress.

DAPHNE
And a hat?

CLAUDETTE looks as if she is going to change her mind. VALERIE gives her a sharp but discreet shove in the ribs.

CLAUDETTE
I'll wear a hat.

DAPHNE is delighted; she beams at the girls.

DAPHNE
Val, call Dr. Harris. Tell her I'll be in to see her tomorrow! The Lord is good. Girls, I'll go get my hats!

DAPHNE exits with a new-found bounce in her step! The sisters watch her with amusement. Lights go down.

Lights up on CLAUDETTE, *who is busy trying on a bunch of awful-looking hats under* DAPHNE's *watchful yet excited eye. There is fun, happy music playing. The atmosphere is fun and there seems to be a new lightness to the exchange with the entire family.*

DAPHNE

The one with the red bow looks better. It's my favourite hat, but I don't mind, Claudette; I'll let you borrow it for Sunday!

CLAUDETTE

But, Mom, it's your favourite hat.

DAPHNE

I know, but you can wear it. Claudette, don't even borrow it—you can keep it! Wear it every day!

CLAUDETTE looks pained, and VALERIE *is delighted to watch her sister squirm. She teases her even more; she picks up another extreme hat, with bows and lace.*

VALERIE

I think you should have this one as well. The green taffeta works so well with your complexion.

DAPHNE

Maybe Val's right. You are a bit too dark for the red. And green could bring out your colour a bit . . . um I know! I have THE hat for you!

DAPHNE reaches dramatically into a big hat box and proudly pulls out a hat. This is a hat like no other! It is huge, with big pink and white polka dots and a big lace trim. DAPHNE hands CLAUDETTE the hat as if it is the most precious thing that she could possibly give to her. CLAUDETTE puts it on with great trepidation. DAPHNE is beaming; VALERIE can barely contain herself.

Now that is what you call a HAT!! Boy, you favour Momma in dat hat. Spitting image of your grandmother. You girls are too young to remember how Momma wouldn't go anywhere without her hat. Even to sell at the market she would have on her fancy hat. Her favourite one was the cream one that Auntie Joyce gave her.

CLAUDETTE
No, her favourite one was the blue one Uncle Roy gave her.

DAPHNE
No. Her favourite one was the one Joyce gave her. She loved it!

CLAUDETTE
No. It was the one Uncle Roy gave her; she wore that one everywhere. She used to tell everyone that it was her favourite hat.

DAPHNE
You were too little to remember anything and I know that Momma's favourite—

Tension begins to rise and everyone feels it. The music abruptly stops.

CLAUDETTE
I know what I remember.

VALERIE can sense the tension in the room and desperately tries to diffuse it.

VALERIE
Well . . . this hat is nice. What about this one, Claude? This one's nice, right, Mom?

CLAUDETTE
This is stupid. I don't want to wear a stupid hat anyways.

CLAUDETTE grabs the hat off her head and starts to quickly stuff it into its box.

DAPHNE
Well you can't go to church without wearing a hat.

CLAUDETTE
Says who?

DAPHNE
It's just the way it is. And I don't need you to embarrass me in front of my church sisters.

CLAUDETTE
If I wear a hat or not, you're going to feel embarrassed once they all find out, and you know they all know anyways. You know they know?

DAPHNE quickly busies herself with putting away the hats and deliberately ignores CLAUDETTE's question.

DAPHNE
Every woman needs to wear a hat to church. So please make sure you choose one for Sunday morning.

CLAUDETTE
Mom, how can you pretend—

DAPHNE
Claudette, I'm tired. Not now.

CLAUDETTE
Mom, I'm tired too. How many nights are you going to pray for me until you just give up, huh?

DAPHNE

A mother doesn't give up on her children.

CLAUDETTE

Really?

DAPHNE picks up a few of the hat boxes and turns to leave.

DAPHNE

Val, make sure you turn down the heat before you leave.

CLAUDETTE

Mom, don't do this. Please will you just talk to me! Or just look at me please . . .

DAPHNE keeps walking firmly towards the door. CLAUDETTE runs ahead and positions herself in the exit, blocking DAPHNE's exit.

MOM, LOOK AT ME! *(gently)* Please.

DAPHNE

Look at what! What you've done with your life? Claudette, you were not raised like this! And I don't know if it's all of those white people at work who make you think this is okay, but it's not! It's not right! You're sinning!

Beat.

And I don't know if somebody put something in your food or maybe you just want to hurt and destroy me! But whatever it is you have done enough! And it is time to STOP this foolishness!

CLAUDETTE

Foolishness? That's how you see it?

DAPHNE

What I see is that you think the world owes you something. That you think how you were raised just wasn't good enough! That being a woman wasn't good enough! Me, your sister, your life just isn't good enough for you. So you had to move away from your family, stop speaking to your mother and nobody knows if you're dead or alive! You cut off all your hair. Don't want to wear a hat! Don't want to wear a dress! You think you need to start acting like a man instead of trying to get one! And I don't understand this! But what I do know is you weren't raised like that and I won't have IT in my house!

CLAUDETTE
Well if you won't have IT in your house, what am I doing here?

VALERIE
Claude, please don't—

CLAUDETTE
Do you want me here or not?

> CLOE *suddenly enters the room as* CLAUDETTE *and* DAPHNE *engage in an intense stare down.* CLOE *begins to sing. The women all sense her presence.* CLAUDETTE *covers her ears as* CLOE's *singing gets louder and then becomes softer as she walks towards* DAPHNE. VALERIE *watches, mesmerized, seeing* CLOE *for the first time.*

Mom, I need to know if you want me here.

> *Two beats.*

Why did you send for us? Huh? You already had your perfect little family, and you knew that Cloe's dad didn't want us here.

DAPHNE
Claudette, that is water under the bridge. And that is that!

CLAUDETTE
Oh of course. We won't talk about how crappy he treated us. How he barely spoke to us, couldn't stand the sight of us. If he thought we ate too much he would tell us to go look for our father and make him support us. And if we didn't

eat, we were wasting his hard-earned food. And let's not talk about how he hid his food in your bedroom closet because he didn't want your damn kids to eat it!

DAPHNE
I left him.

CLAUDETTE
No. He LEFT you after Cloe died. Because there was nothing you had left to keep him around. So you didn't leave him.

DAPHNE
What would you have liked me to have done, Claudette? Tell me! Put you, Valerie, and sick as Cloe was, should I have put you all on my back and go where? Tell me!

CLAUDETTE
You should have never sent for us. We were happy with Momma. We didn't want to come here! You didn't want us. You never wanted us! You should have left us in Jamaica!

> *DAPHNE is taken aback but recovers quickly and straightens her back. She looks to VALERIE, who avoids her eyes, and then she looks back to CLAUDETTE. CLOE starts singing the lullaby. CLOE walks closer to DAPHNE and starts to sing louder. DAPHNE shakes her head as if wanting to drown out the singing. The tension is too much and the noise is too much.*

DAPHNE
You're right, Claudette!!! As ungrateful as you are, I should have never sent for you!! NEVER! I should have left you right there!

> *CLOE's singing stops abruptly. DAPHNE exits the room. CLOE follows immediately behind her.*

> *Blackout.*

> *Intermission.*

ACT TWO

Lights up in CLAUDETTE *and* VALERIE's *childhood room. This is a simple room with two single beds, teddy bears and posters of '80s idols such as Michael Jackson, Prince and Madonna. Time seems to have stood still in this room.* CLAUDETTE *sits on the bed, suitcase half packed. She stops for a minute and picks up the phone. She starts to dial a number and then hangs up. She dials the number again and listens to the voice say "hello" and then hangs up again.* VALERIE *walks into the room and catches her.* CLAUDETTE *guiltily looks away.*

VALERIE
Who you talking to?

CLAUDETTE
No one.

VALERIE
You were on the phone and then you hung it up.

CLAUDETTE
Yep. No big deal, okay.

VALERIE
It was her, wasn't it? Jenna?

CLAUDETTE

It was stupid of me to call but I just wanted to hear her voice. She has this cute way of saying "hello." It's like, "Hello." Not a question like "hello?" But it's more like a final statement. It's like, "Hello." You hear the difference?

VALERIE looks at her likes she's mad.

VALERIE

You've got it bad.

CLAUDETTE laughs.

So what did she say?

CLAUDETTE

Nothing. I just wanted to hear her voice. Hear her say hello because I had forgotten what she sounded like, and I don't want to forget her so I just needed to hear her.

VALERIE nods and suddenly spots the suitcase. CLAUDETTE avoids her eyes.

VALERIE

You're leaving?

CLAUDETTE

Yep.

VALERIE

No talking it through, no goodbyes? This feels familiar. So should I expect a call in the next three years? Five? Or maybe depending on how hurt you are maybe ten!

CLAUDETTE

You know I hate goodbyes. And I was going to call you from the airport, I swear.

VALERIE gives her a pointed look.

VALERIE
You promised . . .

> *CLAUDETTE ignores her and starts quickly throwing clothes in the suitcase, avoiding VALERIE. It is obvious that she is upset but trying to control her emotions.*

CLAUDETTE
You know me and Jenna, we used to dance in the kitchen, the elevator, in the bathroom. We had a walk-in closet and sometimes we would dance in the closet. We used to joke—two lesbians dancing in the closet.

> *She laughs.*

No music or nothing. She would grab me, hold me tight or I would spin her around and we would just start to dance for no reason. And I would make up silly songs and sing them to her. And we would laugh and laugh . . . Our favourite song was um . . . um . . . Oh what was it? Oh my God, I can't believe I can't remember, it was so funny . . . um . . .

VALERIE
I'm sure you'll remember it another time.

CLAUDETTE
No I need to remember it now! It was . . .

> *She starts to sing a tune but it's obvious she has forgotten the words yet tries to sing it anyway.*

She's so beautiful and . . . Um . . . she's so beautiful and um . . . funny . . . doesn't have a lot of money but she's so . . . um beautiful? Damn, what was it!

> *CLAUDETTE becomes visibly upset and agitated.*

I'm starting to forget. And I don't want to forget!

Beat.

Like how does she like her coffee? One sugar? Two? Was it her lower tooth that was chipped, or was it the front one. Her smell. What side of her lip she bit on when she was mad. Was it the left? The right. She never wore lipstick and she had beautiful lips.

Beat.

You would have liked her.

VALERIE
She sounds amazing.

CLAUDETTE
She is.

Two beats.

And I can't believe I'm forgetting stuff about her. I just can't. 'Cause I need to remember. I have to remember.

VALERIE
If it's in the past why do you still need to remember it now?

CLAUDETTE
You just can't forget people who are important to you. You can't forget them! That's not okay. So I just want to remember, okay?

VALERIE
It's funny how people remember things differently.

Two beats.

Because everything you remember about her is always bad.

CLAUDETTE
You don't remember because you were too young and you had me to look after you. But she was a lousy mom. The only person she ever loved was herself, and Cloe. For six years she forgot about us and left us and thought it would be okay to pick up where she left us and it's not. And that's not a memory, it's a fact!

VALERIE
Well here's some more facts! Do you remember the first winter that we got here? She had one pair of tennis shoes. And before she left for work at night she would stuff them with newspaper to keep her feet warm. That was the same winter you got two pairs of matching mittens, a scarf, hat and boots. Do you remember that, Claudette? Or you don't want to remember that?

CLAUDETTE
I—

VALERIE
Or do you remember the time when you insisted for your high-school graduation that you had to have a three-hundred-dollar dress and she couldn't afford it and so she got another job, on top of the other two that she had, sewing shoes from home; her fingers used to bleed and she kept on sewing so she could get the fucking money to buy you your dress. Do you remember that!

CLAUDETTE picks up her suitcase and slams it shut.

CLAUDETTE
I got a plane to catch.

VALERIE
You've always got some place to go, don't you? No wonder Jenna left you, because no one can ever do enough for you! Love you in the way you need to be loved! It's never enough for you, is it?

CLAUDETTE

Don't bring Jenna into this, okay!

VALERIE

Now you're all weepy because you want to remember a damn song that you use to sing to her but when you were with her it wasn't enough, was it? *(mimics CLAUDETTE)* "Something was missing." Something's always missing! No one can do enough! You're like this deep dark empty big hole that no one can ever fill. And it's the same thing with Mom. No matter what she did, or how she tried to love you, something was always missing . . . You don't let anyone in to love you, not even me!

CLAUDETTE

That's not true. I—

VALERIE

Really? If that's not true, why ain't you at home right now in your new house with Jenna? Oh and let's not forget the girl before Jenna. And Keith. You broke up with him five days after he proposed!

CLAUDETTE

I-I wasn't ready for that kind of commitment.

VALERIE

Please! Any time someone shows you that they want you or need you . . . you run. You've never gotten over the fact that she left you behind. And you're so damn worried that everyone is going to leave you that you leave before they leave you!

Two beats.

And now you're leaving once again. 'Cause she's dying and that means she's leaving and God forbid you can allow someone to leave you again!

Beat.

Your mother is dying and that's just a little too needy for you. And yeah this time when she leaves she really isn't coming back . . . So you wanna leave before she does? Sure. Go! Do what you do best! Leave!

An intense stare down occurs between the two sisters. The moment is suddenly broken by CLAUDETTE, *who moves away and grabs her suitcase off the bed before turning with tears in her eyes to look at* VALERIE.

CLAUDETTE
She doesn't want me—

(catches herself) She doesn't want me here. She doesn't want me in her house.

VALERIE
She never said that.

CLAUDETTE *looks at her in disbelief and sadly shakes her head, fighting back tears.*

CLAUDETTE
She doesn't have to.

Lights go down.

Lights up. The same day. VALERIE *and* DAPHNE *are eating dinner in the kitchen.*

DAPHNE
Sister Marie called. Last night she had to take Tamara to the hospital. False labour. They were at the hospital for over seven hours and that poor woman had to get back up again with her tired self to go to work the next morning. Those children won't stop until they kill her.

VALERIE
I'm sure Tamara just didn't fake her labour pains.

DAPHNE
Well the doctor did say, it was false labour, so what does that tell you? Labour or no labour, that child has no business dragging her poor mother through this. Sixteen and a belly! Disgraceful.

VALERIE
Mom, you were about the same age when you had Claudette.

DAPHNE
Times were different then.

    Beat.

I wanted to get out of Poppa house so badly that the first man who offered me a candy I took it. Pity is he wanted to give me more than candy and I was too young to know any better.

VALERIE

After you had Claudette you moved out of Poppa's house and went with Daddy?

DAPHNE

Move where? Where was he going to put me? He lived with his mother and seven brothers and sisters. He had a sweet mouth and that's all he had. Promising the moon and stars, and when it came down to it arms and legs too short to grab the moon.

VALERIE

So what did you do?

> *Unbeknownst to the women,* CLAUDETTE *is at the kitchen door with her suitcase in hand. She listens to the private conversation between* DAPHNE *and* VALERIE.

DAPHNE

Hid Claudette from Poppa for months. He didn't even know I was pregnant. I knew that if he ever found out he would kill me and the baby.

VALERIE

So what about when she was born?

DAPHNE

Five months she was a secret. Your auntie Joyce would keep watch at the end of the hill and when she would see Poppa coming from work she would run, run quick to warn me. And Momma would take Claudette and put her in this little basket behind the house right beside the chicken coop. That's why I can't understand why she's a vegetarian because she's always loved chicken. She used to play with the chickens!

> DAPHNE *laughs to herself.*

And all us girls would take our time and sneak out to watch her.

VALERIE

Momma knew and never told Poppa?

DAPHNE

Not everything you tell a man. And Momma had many secrets. Secrets which turned her into a bitter, hard woman and that's why I knew I had to get you and Claudette out of that house.

She sighs.

And Momma knew Poppa would beat her and me if he ever found out . . . Not that he ever needed a reason to hit her. Once the liquor took hold of him he was a different man.

VALERIE

Poppa use to beat Momma?

DAPHNE

Ten children plus two outside kids. No money. No food. No work. What else could he do? Need something to make you feel like a man.

Two beats.

The only time I ever saw Poppa laugh was when he had a rum bottle in his hand. Help him forget. At the beginning of the bottle he was always happy, could tell the biggest jokes and sing the best songs. Boy, Poppa could sing. He had a dream to be a singer, you know. But I guess it never work out.

VALERIE

Claudette told me that Poppa used to sing to her all the time.

DAPHNE looks shocked by this and confused.

DAPHNE

No. Never. Poppa died before you were even born, so she would be too small to remember Poppa.

She thinks about it and then shakes her head as if this is indeed impossible.

But he did have this beautiful bass voice. He would call me to sit at his foot when he started to sing. He would say, Daphne, come sing with me. I was his favourite, you know; he told everybody. He would say: Daphne may not have the looks, because she favour her mother, but what she have is common sense. Common sense, like her poppa. Poppa always use to say—

VALERIE / DAPHNE
Make sense out of nonsense! No book can teach you common sense!

They both laugh.

DAPHNE
And he would sing. We used to laugh and sing. And by the time he reached the end of that bottle he was the meanest man you ever could know. Us kids would hide from him. And the only one who would deal with him was Momma. Took his anger, his dirty words, all his filth . . . she took it to protect us. Dat's what mother's do.

VALERIE
Who told him about Claudette?

DAPHNE sighs softly and shakes her head.

DAPHNE
One night I was trying to feed her behind the chicken coop. All day she just refused to eat. And she was fussy. She wouldn't tek mi milk and I could hear Poppa calling me. "Daphne, come and sing with me. Come sing nah. Where is dat girl?" And your auntie Joyce and auntie Iona told him that they would sing with him, but he said, "No, I want mi Daphne. Where is she?" And Joyce run out of the house and she say, "Come, Daphne; come now, Poppa needs you . . . "

And I just couldn't leave her in the dark, hungry and crying. I couldn't . . . So I stayed with her. And Poppa start to get mad, start looking everywhere for me. And then him find me. Me and Claudette.

Two beats.

And him just look at me, and he had this sad look in his eye . . . and he said, "Daphne, whose black baby is dis?" And I said mine. Poppa, she's mine.

VALERIE
Did he beat you?

DAPHNE
No, I wish he did. That would have been easier. He just shook his head and kept staring at me and then back at Claudette and then back at me, and he said, "If you don't go inside a chicken coop, chicken can't shit pun you."

Two beats.

"Bring her inside." And after that he never ever really looked at me again. He never asked me to sing with him again . . .

VALERIE
So what happened to—?

DAPHNE
Enough, Valerie. I tired. And cha, I don't have time to be dwelling on all of those t'ings.

She gets up and starts dishing out a plate of food.

Claudette not coming down to eat? She always loves my stew peas. No pig tail, but that's how she likes it.

DAPHNE laughs to herself.

VALERIE

Mom, she's leaving.

DAPHNE

Leaving to go where, at this time of night?

VALERIE

Montreal. She's going home.

DAPHNE

Nonsense, this is her home!

VALERIE

She thinks you don't want her here.

> *DAPHNE says nothing. She puts the plate of food on the table and begins to clear the dishes but you can see that she is holding back her emotions. She starts humming softly as CLOE enters the room. CLOE reaches for her hand and the two of them start to hum the same tune. Their voices become one and seem to take over the room. VALERIE tries to speak over their rising voices.*

I told her that's not true. 'Cause it's not true, right? You need to talk to her tell her to stay and tell her it's not true. Talk to her, Mom!

DAPHNE

Me to talk to her about what? I am sure that I am the mother and she is the child—

VALERIE

Mom, you need to tell her that you want her. That you want her here. Mom, you need—

> *DAPHNE slams the down plate on the table. CLOE immediately stops singing.*

DAPHNE

Tell her that I want her! I carried her for nine months! Pushed her out all on mi own! Take the food out of mi own mouth to feed her. Carry you, me, her, Cloe and the whole world pun mi back! I've done everything and anything! Turned nothing into something for you girls! For what! Huh? For what! What more do you girls want from me? What! Tell me! *(softly)* I need to tell Claudette I need her? Need her now for what?

> *CLOE, as if summoned, sings a slow, haunting tune. CLAUDETTE enters slowly behind CLOE. DAPHNE hears CLOE singing. She looks at CLOE, mesmerized by her and the music. DAPHNE does not appear to see CLAU-DETTE. CLOE reaches out her hand to DAPHNE. DAPHNE hesitates but begins to reach for her, but the mood is abruptly broken by CLAUDETTE, who places her suitcase firmly and loudly on the ground.*

CLAUDETTE

Um . . . I couldn't find a flight. Is it okay if I stick around for a bit?

> *DAPHNE looks at her sadly. Looks as if she wants to say something but can't find the right words.*

> *Two beats.*

DAPHNE

Your dinner's on the table. Stew peas, your favourite.

> *CLOE abruptly leaves the room.*

> *CLAUDETTE silently nods. A relieved VALERIE rushes to the fridge to pour CLAUDETTE a drink.*

> *Lights go down.*

Lights up. Ladies come in dancing before the scene starts. It's two weeks later. DAPHNE, CLAUDETTE and VALERIE walk through the front door. It is obvious they are back from church. DAPHNE looks visibly weaker but trying to hold on.

DAPHNE
Pastor Thomas outdid himself today! What a great sermon!

VALERIE
Indeed! Mom, have something to eat before you get ready for evening service. Sister June said to let you know that they have put you on the top of their prayer list for tonight.

DAPHNE
Nice of them. Very nice. But I think I'm just going to rest tonight.

VALERIE
Mom, you never miss an evening service. You feeling okay?

DAPHNE
Yes. The old girl is just tired. I'm going to read my Bible and go to bed. Not too hungry tonight. Mouth feeling dry though. Val, could you get me a glass of water?

VALERIE
Yes, I'll get it. You sit down.

DAPHNE

It was so nice to have you girls at church with me this morning. Did my heart good. So you girls hurry up and eat and make sure you get to evening service on time. Let them know I truly appreciate all the prayers.

CLAUDETTE

Enough church for me today. I'm wiped.

DAPHNE

One can never have enough church. Church is a good place for young people to be. And it's good for you to be around positive people and away from all of that bad company.

> *VALERIE can see where this is going and tries her best to maintain the peace.*

VALERIE

Um . . . I'll put the kettle on. Mom, tea? Or one of your liquid drinks?

CLAUDETTE

Bad company?

DAPHNE

All of that nonsense in Montreal.

> *VALERIE shoots CLAUDETTE a pleading look and CLAUDETTE decides to heed her silent request.*
>
> *CLAUDETTE sighs.*

CLAUDETTE

I'm going to go—um, watch some TV. Val, send my regrets to the church folks.

DAPHNE

I saw you talking to Brother Elijah after service today. He's a nice guy and . . . single?

The tension slowly rises in the room. VALERIE in her own way tries to diffuse the situation by reaching for one of DAPHNE's liquid drinks.

VALERIE
Okay. Chocolate. Here you go, Mom!

CLAUDETTE
Good for him.

DAPHNE
(quickly) Well what about Brother Michael, Sister Louise's son? Now that's a nice guy for you! In the church and everything. Owns his own home as well!

CLAUDETTE
Not interested. But I'm sure with all that he has going for him he won't be on the market too long.

DAPHNE
Exactly! So that's why you need to grab him! Claudette, you're not a spring chicken anymore. And I've been praying for you. And I would just like to see you settled down with a good husband, a family. Go to service tonight, I know Brother Michael will be there.

CLAUDETTE
Mom, I don't want Michael. I don't want Elijah, okay.

VALERIE
Oops, I forgot the water. Mom, you still want a glass of water?

DAPHNE
Women, we can sometimes be too picky, but Brother Johnathan, he's a lawyer, and you know him and his wife broke up. I heard he's looking to start dating and—

CLAUDETTE
I'm not interested and I think you know that.

VALERIE

Um . . . I think tea would be good. Claudette, tea, coffee?

DAPHNE

God is a forgiving God. Anyone can start over when they desire. And what you were doing in Montreal can just stay there! You're here now, start fresh!

CLAUDETTE

Mom, it doesn't matter if I'm in Brooklyn, Montreal, Jamaica or on the moon. I'm not changing. This is it! This is me!

DAPHNE

Nonsense. You might not know this but . . . I heard *(looks around and whispers)* Brother David, many years ago, was caught up in that same type of life. And he changed himself. Asked God to change him! Now he is married! Him and his wife have a lovely daughter and the wife is pregnant again! He changed because he wanted to and God forgave him!

CLAUDETTE looks at DAPHNE with disbelief and shakes her head.

CLAUDETTE

I'll be upstairs.

CLAUDETTE attempts to leave the room. But DAPHNE is not having it.

DAPHNE

Claudette, you are at the top of my prayers every night. And God spoke to me last night through my dreams. I dreamt that you, Cloe and I were in church and Cloe, she had on this beautiful white dress—she was so beautiful—and Cloe, she poured water over you to baptize you and there was no water left to give you a blessing. And I started to bawl. Cloe give her a blessing and she tried to—

CLAUDETTE

I don't want to hear about Cloe! When are you going to talk about me? I'm living! And I'm right here! Blessing or no blessing but I'm here!

CLAUDETTE and DAPHNE face each other. DAPHNE seems to be conflicted and it appears as if DAPHNE is going to reach out to her, but her focus shifts from CLAUDETTE as she hears CLOE, who enters the room humming, singing low.

DAPHNE
Claudette, you're my child and a mother only wants what best for her child.

CLAUDETTE
This HERE is my best! This is it! This is all I got for you, Mom. And I need you to tell me that what I've got is good enough for you! That there's enough here for you to love.

DAPHNE looks sadly at CLAUDETTE as CLOE begins to sing louder. DAPHNE turns away from CLAUDETTE and begins to walk towards CLOE.

Mom, please. You know I'm not changing. And I need you to love all of me like you love Cloe, please . . .

DAPHNE abruptly turns around and CLOE's singing becomes softer.

DAPHNE
Claudette, I-I-I just can't accept this. I won't. I can't. The Bible clearly states that—

CLAUDETTE
This isn't about the Bible! For God's sake! Stop hiding behind your god-damn Bible!

CLOE's singing stops. The air is charged. DAPHNE looks as if she has been slapped across the face. Everyone watches as DAPHNE charges across the room to face CLAUDETTE. She is so close to CLAUDETTE it appears as if she may hit her.

DAPHNE
I beg your pardon! What did you say? How dare you!

Beat.

Whatever kind of so-called life you are choosing to live, you can live! But I will not tolerate your blasphemy in my house. Do you understand! Do I make myself clear! Not in MY HOUSE! Never!

DAPHNE shoots her a look of disgust. She is shaking with anger and close to hitting CLAUDETTE. She looks from VALERIE to CLAUDETTE in sheer disbelief. CLOE's singing starts again softly and slowly swells. Suddenly the phone rings. The women look from each other to the phone, the ringing persistent. VALERIE reaches to answer it.

VALERIE
Hello.

Beat.

Oh my goodness! Calm down, Sister Marie, we'll be right there. Don't worry. Mount Sinai, we're on our way!

VALERIE hangs up the phone and quickly grabs her coat.

Tamara is in labour. It's not looking good. It's breech. She lost a lot of blood, and the cord is around the baby's neck. They're not sure if she or the baby is going to make it. Claudette, let's go! Mom, we'll call you from the hospital!

DAPHNE
What! Sister Marie needs me! Her child is having a child— Let's go!

DAPHNE quickly puts on her coat and hat and heads to the door first before the girls.

Valerie, grab my Bible!

All three women rush out of the door.

Lights down on stage.

The next scene switches from past to present, dreamlike. Voices are heard in the blackness. Despite the dreamlike atmosphere, there is a sense of urgency in the room. Various voices are high-pitched and overlapping. The voices are mixed with music and soft singing. This space is the in-between purgatory where CLOE *resides, between dream and reality.*

UNKNOWN VOICE
Push!

UNKNOWN VOICE 2
I can't.

UNKNOWN VOICE
You have to do it for the baby!

Daphne, push!

UNKNOWN VOICE 2
My baby, please help my baby.

UNKNOWN VOICE
Push!

The baby's coming!

I think we might be losing her.

Push. Come on, one more, Tamara, one more! Daphne, one more!

UNKNOWN VOICE 2
I'm tired. Please.

UNKNOWN VOICE
Push, come on, for the baby. For the baby! Daphne, push! Tamara, push!

UNKNOWN VOICE 2
I can't! I'm . . .

UNKNOWN VOICE
Do it for your baby!

It's a girl!

UNKNOWN VOICE 2
Take the baby!

UNKNOWN VOICE
Hide the baby!

Lights down.

Lights up on stage three weeks later. CLAUDETTE *is heading out, loaded down with baby stuff.* VALERIE *glances up from where she sits at the kitchen table reading a magazine.*

VALERIE

Going to the hospital again? How the baby doing?

CLAUDETTE

They said that she will be in ICU for a few more weeks but she's getting better every day. She's three weeks old but so tiny. But she's a fighter.

VALERIE

How's Tamara? How she doing with all of this?

CLAUDETTE

Overwhelmed. I thought it would be better that she stay away. Especially now that's she's deciding to give the baby up for adoption.

VALERIE

So she's not keeping it.

CLAUDETTE

Nope. And she's struggling with that decision. But I've told her that sometimes as a mom you got to do what's best for your child. Sometimes you have to make hard decisions.

VALERIE

Yeah, decisions that sometimes others don't understand . . .

She looks pointedly at CLAUDETTE.

CLAUDETTE

This is not the same. Tamara is sixteen, she can't raise a child. She's a child herself.

VALERIE

Mom was seventeen when she had you.

There is a brief silence as CLAUDETTE *seems to really start to think about this.*

So what's going to happen to that poor little baby?

CLAUDETTE

I know this may sound crazy but I've already spoken to Tamara about it and I know you wanted a baby . . . so I thought maybe you could take her!

VALERIE

Claude!

CLAUDETTE

Val, think about it for a minute. It's a win-win! You want to be a mom, she wants to know her kid is going to be okay, and I'll help. This would be amazing for everyone!

VALERIE

And what am I supposed to tell my husband? Oh, David, I just dropped by Mount Sinai and picked up a little black baby. What am I? Angelina Jolie!

CLAUDETTE

For once think about what you want, NOT David, and yeah, the timing is quicker than planned, but you're trying to have a kid and now you got one!

VALERIE

Correction. We were trying to have a baby.

Two beats.

VALERIE sighs.

Last week's session was the first time our therapist and me finally agreed on something. David is moving out and we're getting a divorce.

Beat.

We're both in love with someone who we used to be. I'm not a frightened little girl who needs someone to take care of me anymore.

CLAUDETTE
Are you sure? Val, maybe take a bit more time or see another therapist, but don't rush into something that you may regret.

VALERIE
I knew this months ago. But I guess saying it aloud just makes it real. And I wasn't ready to make it real. But this whole thing with Mom, and you coming back, just made me start to do some thinking. Time is too precious. And I need to let go. Let go of the past and find some place to forgive David. When you forgive it allows you to truly live . . .

VALERIE looks pointedly at CLAUDETTE, who gives her a quick hug and glances at her watch.

CLAUDETTE
I got to get to the hospital. You wanna come? It might cheer you up. She's so cute; she's already put on four ounces. Val, you should see her!

VALERIE
Mom had a bad night. I think it's best that someone's here with her. She was asking for you last night.

CLAUDETTE looks guilty.

CLAUDETTE

I just think it's best that we keep out of each other's way, and I've been at the hospital a lot. But I'll check in on her tonight.

VALERIE
She'll like that.

> CLAUDETTE *nods and heads out.* VALERIE *looks longingly at the closed door.*

> *Lights down.*

Lights come up on DAPHNE *on the sofa. She is reading the Bible aloud but struggling.* CLAUDETTE *gently takes it from her and begins to read it.* DAPHNE *is visibly weaker but holding strong.* VALERIE *is busy doing dishes at the sink.*

CLAUDETTE
For us to enter the kingdom of God we must be childlike.

DAPHNE
Lord, I'm ready. That was a good scripture, Claudette.

Beat.

Val, can I get that tea, please.

VALERIE hurries over with a teapot and pours. CLAUDETTE *helps* DAPHNE *up and adjusts her pillow. Both of them start fussing over* DAPHNE.

Okay, okay, enough now! Lord, when you have your kids you're not thinking that one day they will come to take care of you. Thank God I have you girls to take care of me. Look at poor Sister Marie now with that little Tamara and another mouth to feed. How is she going to manage?

VALERIE
She's not keeping it.

DAPHNE
What! So what is going to happen to that poor little baby?

CLAUDETTE

I'm taking her. Tamara said that I could have her.

There is a stunned silence in the room. VALERIE *suddenly reaches out and hugs* CLAUDETTE.

VALERIE

Oh my goodness. Congrats!

DAPHNE *is visibly upset and in shock. She looks at them with disbelief.*

DAPHNE

You two stop this nonsense! This is a child we are talking about. Not some dolly you pass around. Having a child is a big responsibility and, Claudette, your life is DEFINITELY not ready for all of that right now.

CLAUDETTE

What do you mean my life is not ready right now?

A nervous VALERIE *musters the courage to jump in and for once seems to be taking charge with* DAPHNE *in order to defend* CLAUDETTE.

VALERIE

Um . . . I think Claudette will make a great mother and um . . . it's her decision and we should support her and that's that. *(firmly)* Now, Mom, drink your tea before it gets cold.

DAPHNE *looks at* VALERIE *as if seeing her for the first time. Shocked but determined,* DAPHNE *pushes on.*

DAPHNE

(firmly) Valerie, I've had enough tea, thanks! As I was saying before I was interrupted, this is not a good idea.

Beat.

I'm sure if Tamara knew all what is going on in your life she wouldn't be comfortable with you raising her child. And a mother needs to—

CLAUDETTE
Wait a minute, you're giving me advice on what it takes to be a mother? You? You who left her children behind?

VALERIE has had enough of both of them and slams her hands down on the table. This is a new and improved VALERIE and the other two are shocked.

VALERIE
Enough, both of you! I'm fed up of this! Can't we just have one night without the two of you arguing!

DAPHNE
I don't know what has gotten into you tonight, Valerie, but please watch your tone with me. I'm not arguing with Claudette. All I'm trying to say is a child should be raised in a good home, with a mother and a father when possible. And Claudette doesn't have that.

She looks clearly at CLAUDETTE.

And the life that you are CHOOSING to live doesn't seem to warrant that. Why bring an innocent child into all of that?

CLAUDETTE
Because I'm gay I can't raise this baby? Well I may be far from ideal in your eyes but let me tell you I would never leave my child. Never! What mother leaves their child? Huh?

VALERIE
Claudette, please calm down. Not now. Not now . . . please not now . . .

CLAUDETTE looks at the two of them in disbelief. CLOE enters the room humming slowly and looking deliberately at CLAUDETTE.

Two beats.

CLAUDETTE *gets emotional to the point of tears.*

CLAUDETTE
You know, last night I was at that hospital and I prayed so hard that Tamara would say that it was okay for me to have her because I knew I could never leave her. Couldn't even bring myself to think about leaving her. She is not even mine and I didn't want to leave her. I've been with her every day since she's been born. I've been her mother! Singing to her, holding her little hand, even praying for her. I've been there just wishing something good for her. Something more than I ever had. I've watched her when she was sleeping. I didn't want to miss a minute, not one moment. And you missed six years?

Two beats.

You packed a suitcase and left. Just left . . . YOU LEFT and didn't look back!

A shaken but newly invigorated DAPHNE *rises from the couch.*

DAPHNE
Do whatever! Because you think a good mother should have stayed, so be it. But let me tell you something. I *wished* for something better for you too! I left because I wanted to give you kids something better than I ever had. I wanted so badly for you to have a life. A better life than I ever had. I left because I never wanted my girls to ever walk in bare feet. I left because I didn't want any of you to miss a day in school because I didn't have the money to pay your school fees or for your books. I left because I didn't want my girls to look up at the sky and pray every day for something better, some way better. I left because I didn't want you to think that you had to lay with every and any man who promised to buy you a new dress to wear to church and you so wanted that new dress that you stayed the night, even when it hurt to stay . . .

I left because I wanted—NO, I needed you girls to know that you could be bigger than a one-room shack on Mandeville Road with nine hungry people in it! I left because I wanted the world to give you a chance. Chances that I never had. Give you choices that I never had.

You two deserved a chance. A bigger chance than I ever got! It was never for me . . . Never for me . . . Never! You were my children, my two little girls. And no mother ever wants to leave her children. No mother, but every mother wants better for her children than herself. So, Claudette, you're right, it may not have been the choice you would have made . . . but for me you were my only choice!

> DAPHNE *looks at them with pain in her eyes, pleading with them to understand.*

> DAPHNE *and* CLAUDETTE *look at each other.* CLAUDETTE *looks at* DAPHNE *as if seeing her for the first time.* CLOE *watches the women with hope in her eyes.* CLAUDETTE *is visibly shaken with tears in her eyes.* DAPHNE *looks visibly weakened; she leans over on the table and starts to shake and cry.* VALERIE *rushes to her side.* CLAUDETTE *is unable to deal with this level of emotion from her mother.*

CLAUDETTE
I-I-I'll be at the hospital.

> CLAUDETTE *leaves.* CLOE *starts to sing, but it is more like the cry of a desperate woman.*

> *Lights down.*

Lights up on CLOE *and* DAPHNE. *A dreamlike setting, this is as close to heaven as we can imagine.* CLOE *is reaching out to* DAPHNE, *arms stretched wide open, beckoning for* DAPHNE *to come to her.*

DAPHNE
Mommy is okay. I'm okay. I'm coming soon. But they need me. The girls need me. Just give me a little more time, Cloe. I soon come.

CLOE nods, yet she lingers. She is unsure. A bright spotlight is seen;
CLOE walks towards the light but is hesitant and looks back at DAPHNE.

Momma and Poppa are over there waiting for you, and Auntie Joon. They'll take care of you till I come. Walk towards the light. Walk into the light, darling. Walk. *(whispers)* I love you . . .

CLOE walks bravely into the light and disappears.

Lights fade.

Lights up on DAPHNE *sleeping on the couch.* CLAUDETTE *enters through the door, visibly surprised to see* DAPHNE *on the couch.* DAPHNE *wakes up. She looks at* CLAUDETTE *as if this is the first time she is truly seeing her.*

CLAUDETTE
Sorry, I didn't mean to wake you.

DAPHNE
You didn't. A mother never really sleeps until all her children are safely in the house. Trust me, you'll never get a good night's sleep again.

CLAUDETTE *gets* *defensive.*

CLAUDETTE
I'm not worried about my sleep. I'll be fine.

DAPHNE
You'll be more than fine, Claudette. That I have no doubt about. You're the strong one. From ever since . . .

Beat.

Even when you were little, when Valerie was the one hiding behind my skirt, you were always out front. Leading the way. Never scared.

Beat.

I've always worried about Val. That girl scared of her own shadow, and then Cloe, so sickly that I thought if I held her too tight she would break.

Beat.

But you, I always thought that you just didn't really need me, that you would be okay . . . My brave, strong little girl. Even when I left you girls. You were not bigger than a grasshopper, dusty, ashy bare feet in the red dirt.

She laughs softly to herself.

But there you were . . . Brave and strong, holding Valley's little hand so tightly. And you had tears in your eyes but you wouldn't let them fall, and you said, "Mommy, don't worry. You'll be back soon and I'll look after Val for you."

Beat.

And you did. You always have . . .

Beat.

And now she really need you, now that David and her have mash up!

CLAUDETTE
She told you?

DAPHNE
No. But a mother always knows. Just like I've always known about you . . . prayed on it but I always knew . . .

DAPHNE smiles sadly.

How is the baby doing?

CLAUDETTE

She's good. They let me hold her for the first time tonight. I can't even describe it but it's like—

DAPHNE

I remember the first time I held you. And you looked right back at me with those big bright ackee-seed eyes, didn't even blink. Even back then you weren't afraid to look people in the eye. And you looked at me and you knew I was your mother.

Two beats.

Hard to explain. I guess I'm not making any sense . . . old brain tired now.

CLAUDETTE

You're making sense. When I held her today she looked at me and I knew she had chosen me to be her mother. And I felt like I could do it. That I could do anything. That I was going to be fine, and I know you don't agree but I'm—

DAPHNE

You got Robinson blood running through you. Strong women. We always do what we want to do. Run when everybody is walking. Fly when everybody else is dreaming about it.

Beat.

And you are definitely your mother's daughter, so you're going to be fine. Just fine.

CLAUDETTE smiles gratefully.

So she's a good baby, not fussy?

CLAUDETTE

She was a bit fussy today, but I held her real tight and I whispered, "Mommy loves you," and she stopped crying.

The two women look lovingly at each other. Words are not needed. DAPHNE smiles weakly.

DAPHNE

Claudette, I umm—I—um I want you to know that um . . .

Beat.

I do . . . Um I was thinking that when she comes out of the hospital that you and the baby could stay here.

CLAUDETTE is visibly shaken but happy.

CLAUDETTE

You want me to stay here?

DAPHNE

You're my child.

Two beats.

And where else would my grandchild go? You can roam around the world with a knapsack on your back, eating your tofuee, but my grandchild needs a home. As a matter of fact, what is the name of that pickney?

CLAUDETTE

I was thinking maybe to call her Zoey.

DAPHNE

Zo-what? You have to give her a Biblical name.

Two beats.

I've always liked the name Naomi.

CLAUDETTE
Naomi?

DAPHNE
Remember the Bible story of Ruth and Naomi? It was your favourite Bible verse. The story of the two women together.

Beat.

Ruth and Naomi . . .

> *A knowing look passes between them. The women reach a peaceful understanding. They quote the Bible verse together.*

CLAUDETTE / DAPHNE
"Do not press me to leave you or to turn back from following you. Where you go, I will go; where you lodge, I will lodge; your people shall be my people, and your God my God.

Where you die, I will die—there I will be buried. May the Lord do thus and so to me, and more as well, not even death will part me from you."

> DAPHNE *looks up at* CLAUDETTE, *looks her squarely in the eyes.*

DAPHNE
I will never leave you. Not even death will part me from you . . .

> *Lights down.*

THE END

Trey Anthony is known for the groundbreaking and award-winning television and theatrical production *'da Kink in my hair*. She is the first black Canadian woman to write and produce a television show in prime time on a major Canadian network. Trey is a former television producer for the Women's Television Network (now W) and a writer for the Comedy Network and CTV. She was recently named a Bell Media Fellow, which recognizes emerging television producers and their contribution to Canadian media. She is the creator of the wellness speaking series "A black girl in love with herself." She is regularly invited to schools to speak to students about sexuality, body image and other issues. Originally based in Toronto, Trey now lives in Georgia.

First edition: October 2017
Printed and bound in Canada by Rapido Books, Montreal

Jacket design by Marc Lostracco

**PLAYWRIGHTS
CANADA PRESS**

202-269 Richmond St. W.
Toronto, ON
M5V 1X1

416.703.0013
info@playwrightscanada.com
www.playwrightscanada.com
@playcanpress